Pod Publicity

How to Take a Print-on-Demand Book From Obscurity to Profitability

Heather R. Wallace

Written by Heather R. Wallace. Copyright © 2009 by Heather R. Wallace. All rights reserved worldwide.

No part of this book may be reproduced, distributed, transmitted, sold, or given away, in any form or by any means whatsoever without written permission from the author except in the case of brief quotations embodied in critical articles and reviews.

Every effort has been made to ensure that this book is complete and accurate. The publisher and the author, however, are in no way responsible for any human error, typographical mistakes, or any consequences resulting from the use of this book. The material in this book is provided "as is" without warranty of any kind.

Any trademarks, service marks, or product names mentioned within this book are the property of their respective owners.

ISBN-10: 1448654971
ISBN-13: 9781448654970

Contents

Foreword by Dan Poynter..i
About the Author...v
Introduction...vii
A Bit About Print-on-Demand...1
    Why Print-on-Demand Is the Right Choice...............................3
    CreateSpace and Lulu Versus the Other Guys...........................5
    Should Becoming a Pro Be in Your Plans?...............................7
    POD R-E-S-P-E-C-T..8
Prior to Promotion 11
    Design Your Book for the Online Marketplace..........................12
    You Can't Judge a Book by Its Cover, but Most People Do....12
    What's in a Title? Only Everything....................................15
    And Here's the Pitch..17
Building Your Web Presence..19
    To Blog or Not to Blog...20
    Setting Up Your Site...21
    Make Your Theme Unique to You.......................................26
    Extra! Extra! Create an Online Media Kit All About It.........31
Navigating the Amazon..37
    Pimp Your Book Detail Page..39
    Author Central..41
    Tags..47
    Tag for Amazon Search...48
    Listmania!...49

So You'd Like to...Guides	52
Amapedia	56
Buy X, Get Y	56
Customer Image Gallery	58
Customer Communities	59
Writing Reviews	60
How to Deal with Negative Reviews	61

Getting the Publicity Machine Up and Running......63

The Reviewer Package in Review	64
Publicity Seekers Can Be Choosers	68
Publicity Is a Numbers Game	76
What to Do When You've Found a Keeper	77
First Contact	80
Hi, Remember Me?	84
When POD Publishers and Podcasters Unite	87
Today's Very Special Guest Blogger Is...You	90
Amazon Reviewers	91
Distributing a Press Release Isn't so Pressing	95
Article Marketing	97

Networking Works......103

Carry on a Conversation	104
Commenting on Blogs	105
Social Networks Where Bibliophiles Can Share Books	106
Get Your Readers All A-Twitter	108
Fraternizing in the Forums	110

Alternate Formats......113

Here, There, and Everywhere......117

Appendix 119
Web Site Addresses 119
Index 123

Foreword by Dan Poynter

When I published the first edition of *The Self-Publishing Manual* back in 1979 I never could have imagined how the world of self-publishing would change. Today, absolutely anyone can see their name in print thanks to print-on-demand technology. While print-on-demand does remove many of the hurdles from the publishing process it does not guarantee success.

Many print-on-demand publishers will enjoy the elation of seeing their name in print only to suffer the disappointment of less than stellar sales. That is because simply placing your book in print is not enough to generate results. You may have written a wonderful book, but if no one knows about it, then your efforts will have been for naught. If you want to sell your book, then publicity and marketing are an absolutely vital part of the process.

Succeeding with a print-on-demand title isn't the

impossible task that some would have you believe, but reaching your goals will take effort on your part. What is really required to succeed, as a print-on-demand publisher, is a solid plan of action for your publicity campaign.

That is where *POD Publicity* comes in. In this book, Heather Wallace generously shares the firsthand knowledge that she acquired while publicizing and marketing her own print-on-demand titles. Owning a copy of *POD Publicity* is like having a trusted adviser there to guide you every step of the way toward success. So, for those in need of a plan of action, this book really does serve as an excellent blueprint for success.

After reading Heather's book one thing is clear. Any print-on-demand publisher who is serious about succeeding should arm themselves with a copy of this book. Doing so will make them a force to be reckoned with, because the techniques provided in these pages really do mean the difference between failure or ultimate success.

The fact that you purchased a copy of this book signals that you are serious about succeeding and for that I commend you. Now, get busy reading and then get out there and make success happen.

Dan Poynter
The Self-Publishing Manual

About the Author

Heather Wallace is a writer, blogger, author, and web developer. She began writing as a child and even had some of her early work published in national publications. As an adult, Heather's work has appeared in national, regional, and online publications.

Since 1997, Heather has developed and managed several different web sites and blogs. One of her web sites was featured in several editions of *Que's Internet Yellow Pages* as well as on the television program *She-Commerce*. In addition, one of her blogs had the second fastest growing Google Gadget during the month of March beating out gadgets from powerhouses like The Weather Channel, Windows Live Mail, and Wikipedia Photo of the Day, which were also among the top ten.

Heather is the author of two self-published titles, three print-on-demand books, and three ebooks. Her books have been both well-received by critics and enjoyed by readers.

All of this vast and varied experience has shown Heather what it takes to succeed as a writer. It was never her intention to work a 9-5 job. It took perseverance, hard work, and a little bit of luck, but she was ultimately able to achieve her goals and now enjoys financial freedom while working from the comfort of her own home.

Introduction

The sad fact is that many print-on-demand publishers will be disappointed with their sales figures. This is due, in large part, to the fact that they simply didn't do enough to get the word out about their book. If a buyer hasn't heard of your title, then it will be impossible for them to even consider purchasing it. It is the purpose of this book to help you avoid being one of those disappointed publishers. With the information in these pages you will be able to instead take control of your book's future and ensure that it will be a favorable one.

In order to achieve success with this book it should be noted that you must read it from beginning to end. If you skip from section to section you will miss many important points, some of which are referred to in later chapters. If you really are serious about seeing your book succeed then make the time to read this book and employ the techniques that are presented in its pages.

It is my hope that this book will be the cornerstone of your title's success. I have included every technique that you need to employ in order take your print-on-demand title from a book that only you, your family, and friends have heard of and transform it into a well-known and profitable title.

Chapter 1

A Bit About Print-on-Demand

As a writer, there are certain accomplishments that feel like no other, and having a book published is certainly one of them. There is nothing so gratifying as holding your own book in your hands and the satisfaction of knowing that others will be reading your work. Years ago, many thought that the only respectable route to achieve that accomplishment was to have your manuscript accepted by a traditional publishing house. For many, that would only ever be a dream.

Sure, there was self-publishing, but it was viewed as an alternate route. Many perceived it poorly and saw it as the last resort of authors who had tried the traditional way of publishing and failed. Little did they realize that self-publishing is actually an excellent first choice for authors. It would take time before self-publishing would finally gain a certain amount of respect and people would begin to see the benefits that it has to offer.

As technology advanced the world of self-publishing also evolved. Self-publishers formerly had to hire a printer and have thousands of dollars worth of books printed in the hope that they would earn back their investment. This was quite a gamble that didn't pay off for many. Now, however, self-publishers can have their book in print with a minimal investment thanks to print-on-demand. Many, however, now have the same poor opinion of print-on-demand that self-publishing formerly suffered. The naysayers haven't stopped to realize just how beneficial print-on-demand can be for those hoping to have their title published. The fact that you are reading this book, however, means that you realize just how beneficial print-on-demand can be for absolutely every author.

Why Print-on-Demand Is the Right Choice

Even today, some might wonder why an author wouldn't just try to go the traditional route and then opt for print-on-demand when all else fails. Well, there are two excellent reasons why authors should avoid both the traditional publishing route and standard self-publishing in favor of print-on-demand. Those two reasons are control and profit.

Let us first examine why print-on-demand trumps the traditional publishing houses. If you go the print-on-demand route, then you will remain in complete control of your title. Can you say the same thing if you sell your manuscript to a publishing house? For example, if a traditional publishing house feels that sales of your title are languishing, then they have every right to cease publishing your title. Alternatively, as a print-on-demand publisher your title will never go out of print unless, for some reason, you decide to stop selling it. Also, the royalty that you will receive from a publishing house will be a pittance compared to the amount of money that you receive on the sale of each title as a POD publisher.

Now, what about standard self-publishing? Why should you choose print-on-demand instead. The answer is easy. With print-on-demand the investment required to get started is minor compared to self-publishing. As was mentioned, to begin self-publishing you would have to invest thousands of dollars in inventory. That is not the case with print-on-demand. Also, as a self-publisher you have to handle distribution. Conversely, print-on-demand companies deal with all of those headaches for you. Those are just two of the many reasons why print-on-demand is so much more attractive than going the standard self-publishing route.

When all of the pros and cons are examined

print-on-demand really is a no lose option for authors who want to see their book in print. Now that you can see why print-on-demand is the best choice you must next decide which company to choose as your printer.

CreateSpace and Lulu Versus the Other Guys

With so many print-on-demand companies to choose from your first decision as a POD publisher will be which one to select. Little time needs to be given to this decision, however, as CreateSpace and Lulu are the obvious choices. As of this writing, both of these POD publishers allow authors to publish their titles absolutely free. Well, okay, not entirely free because you will have to pay for a proof copy, but I can tell you that the price of a proof copy is peanuts compared to the prices that the other companies charge to get your book printed and distributed.

Which of these publishers that you choose will depend upon a number of factors. First, calculate the profit margins and determine which of the two will allow for a greater profit. Next, look at the benefits provided with their free packages and determine which offers more desirable perks. Fully investigate both services before making a decision between the two because it is better to choose the right publisher the first time rather than dealing with switching companies later on.

It should be noted that if you live outside the United States, then Lulu will be your only option as CreateSpace currently doesn't offer its services to those located outside the US.

So, the long and short of it is that both CreateSpace and Lulu are a much less expensive way for authors to have their book published and distributed. Now, while CreateSpace and Lulu are the obvious choices you may, for your own reasons, have your heart set on a different publisher. If that is the case, then that is your choice. Rest assured that all of the promotion techniques mentioned in this book can be applied no matter which print-on-demand publisher you choose.

Should Becoming a Pro Be in Your Plans?

CreateSpace offers a Pro Plan which does cost money if you want to reap the benefits, but the plan is entirely optional and certainly not required for success. The Pro Plan allows subscribers to earn higher profits on the sale of each title and, also, to purchase copies of their own books at a lower price. Whether you should sign-up for the Pro Plan right away depends on one factor. If you plan to send physical review copies, which I don't recommend, then you should sign-up right away. If, however, you opt to send ebook review copies, then it is best to wait on the Pro Plan.

The Pro Plan does offer some very attractive benefits and I highly recommend it, but not in the beginning. It is best to keep your expenses as low as possible at this stage. It is at this time that you will be able to gauge the success of your title. Once you find that sales are coming in, then that would be a good time to upgrade to the Pro Plan.

POD R-E-S-P-E-C-T

You may be worried that becoming a POD publisher will automatically ruin your chances at success because you are concerned that people won't take you seriously. Well, I am here to tell you that your title will not suffer because it is published via print-on-demand.

Neither reviewers nor customers are going to care that you went the print-on-demand route. When I contacted potential reviewers for one of my titles only one turned me away saying that they only reviewed books from publishing houses. As for customers, if you write something that they want to read, then they will buy regardless of how the book was published. Evidence of this can be found on the Amazon product page for one of my print-on-demand titles. On that page is a section titled "What Do Customers Ultimately Buy After Viewing This Item?" There it says that 93% of the visitors to my book's product page purchased my title versus 7% who purchased a competing title by a very well-known figure whose book was published by a large publishing house. That means that the large majority of customers choose my book over a well-known figure without a second thought that it was published via print-on-demand.

So, as you can see, print-on-demand doesn't really suffer from the stigma that some would have you believe. Publishing your title via print-on-demand will not harm your chances with reviewers and it will not cost you customers.

Chapter 2

Prior to Promotion

Since the focus of this book is primarily on publicity for print-on-demand titles, and not on writing the book itself, I will only touch on a few things that should be considered before the promotion process begins. It is important that these topics are addressed, however, as they will greatly impact the success that you will have during the promotion phase. In some instances, the topics discussed in this chapter could quite possibly make or break your promotional efforts so particular attention should be given to each of these items.

Design Your Book for the Online Marketplace

It's a simple fact that, as a print-on-demand publisher, the majority of your books are going to be sold online. This is especially true if you publish with CreateSpace as your book will be solely distributed through Amazon and Target. For this reason it is vital that you design your book for the online marketplace. Customers will not be able to pick up your book and leaf through it. That means that you have to use elements like your cover, title, and back cover copy to grab their attention, draw them in, and convert them from browser to buyer.

You Can't Judge a Book by Its Cover, but Most People Do

As the saying goes, "You only get one chance to make a first impression." It is your cover that makes that first impression by signaling your level of professionalism and letting readers know the level of quality that they can expect when reading your book. If your cover is poorly designed then readers won't take you seriously no matter how well-written your book is. Sadly, many probably won't even bother to further investigate your title if your book cover initially turns them off. So, if your book cover creates a poor first impression then it will be an uphill battle for you to make the sale.

Many writers mistakenly think that designing their own cover is the best route because they are looking to save money, but that may not necessarily be the case. If you have artistic ability, then by all means, design your own cover. Just make sure to get feedback from people who will give you an honest opinion. Asking your mom or significant other isn't the best route as they will undoubtedly want to spare your feelings. If your cover gets rave reviews from unbiased individuals, then go ahead and use it.

If you are unable to design a first-class cover on

your own, then outsourcing is a viable option. I have never had much luck with sites such as Elance or Rent a Coder, so I really wouldn't recommend them. Of the projects that I have listed at sites such as these, I have never had a satisfactory outcome. Besides, while you could hire someone from overseas to work for a bargain you will find that copyright laws are not the same from country to country which means that you might encounter difficulties.

If you do opt for having someone else design your cover, then I would recommend crowdsourcing. Further, I would suggest that you list your project as a design contest at 99 Designs (Fig. 1). There you will be able to post your project and set your budget. Designers will then post their design concept for you to evaluate. At 99 Designs you can get some really great work for a reasonable price. Since you will have several designs to choose from, you can easily solicit opinions from others and evaluate your options prior to settling on a cover. In this way, you will be able to

Prior to Promotion

see many different possible covers and choose the one that you like the best.

Fig. 1 - 99 Designs

What's in a Title? Only Everything

The title of your book will have almost as large of an impact on a prospective reader as your cover. It is for this reason that great care should be given to selecting a title. Mundane should be avoided at all costs. You will need to create something memorable that instantly communicates the benefits of your book. You also need to create a sense of intrigue. Make them curious about what your book has to offer. Create a feeling that they simply can't resist knowing what they will read if only they were to buy your book.

Just take a moment to consider the titles of these bestselling books.

- *The 4-Hour Workweek: Escape 9-5, Live Anywhere, and Join the New Rich*
- *Chicken Soup for the Soul*
- *Fix-It and Forget-It Cookbook: Feasting with Your Slow Cooker*
- *Stitch 'N Bitch: The Knitter's Handbook*

What do they all have in common? They are all creative, memorable, and intriguing. Wouldn't you like to know how to have a 4-hour work week? If I were stuck in a 9-5 job, then I certainly would. And you know what? I would really be interested to know how my slow cooker could allow me to fix-it and forget-it. Each of these titles are bestsellers and much of that success can be attributed to a fantastic title. Just imagine what a winning title could do for your book.

And Here's the Pitch

The words that you include on the back of your book have one job and one job only. Their task is to grab the interest of browsers and convince them that they must buy your book. In order to accomplish that objective, you may be tempted to write a sales pitch in which you mention the features that make your book the best in its genre. Doing that, however, would be a mistake. No one likes a sales pitch and the majority of shoppers are not primarily interested in features.

Instead, they want to know how reading your book can benefit them. What is it about your title that will improve their lives? Yes, you can mention features in your back cover copy, but you should never do so without sharing the benefit of that feature as well. By following this technique, you will effectively tell browsers what your book will do for them that the other books won't. Once you have convinced them that your book is more beneficial than the competition then they will be that much more likely to buy your title.

Chapter 3

Building Your Web Presence

For your publicity efforts to be successful, it is vital that you have a web presence. If you are unwilling to take that step then you may as well pack it in now, because, without one, you simply will not be a success. Think of your web site as command central. Your web site will work to sell your book, it will act as a liaison with the media to garner you publicity, and it will allow you to transform yourself from an unknown into someone well-known and respected as an expert in their field.

To Blog or Not to Blog

Now, you may be wondering if you should build a static web site or a blog for your book's web presence. I have done it both ways and I am here to tell you that, while a blog is not absolutely necessary, it comes pretty highly recommended. With a blog you can post regular updates, build an audience, and connect with your readers. Also, you can use your blog to help build your credibility. The content that you post to your site will serve to transform you from an unknown into someone well-known in your field. All of this will help you sell books, which is your ultimate goal.

Now, just because you have a blog, that doesn't mean you have to become a slave to it. I would strongly suggest that you don't overextend yourself when it comes to posting. Your goal in writing your book was most probably to be able to generate passive income and a blog really just flies in the face of all that. Well, in order to sell copies, it is just a fact that you won't be

Building Your Web Presence

able to take a completely passive role. I would say that you only need to update your blog about once or twice a week. That way you can reap the benefits of a blog without working constantly on creating content.

Setting Up Your Site

If I have convinced you that a blog is the way to go, which I will assume that I have, then you will need to set about creating your site.

Fig. 2 - Blogger

You could set-up a free account at Blogger (Fig. 2) or Wordpress.com (Fig. 3) and host your site there, but I would advise against it. If either service decides, for whatever reason, that they simply don't like your site, then they can and will delete it and all of your content will be lost. Blogger does allow users to publish their posts to their own domain, so that is an option.

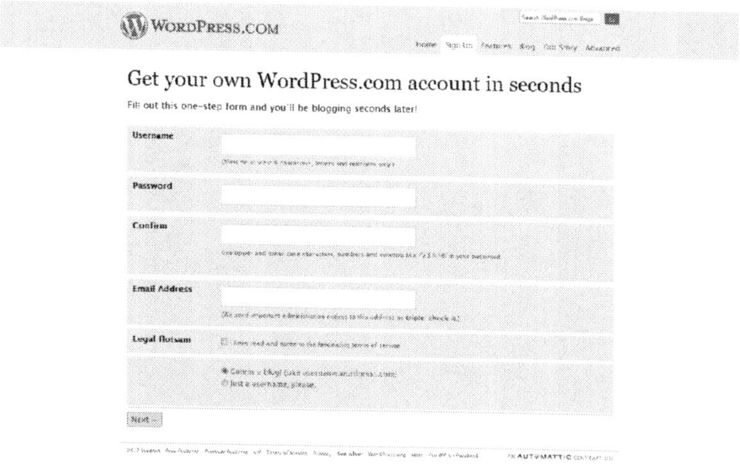

Fig. 3 - Wordpress.com

It is best to remain in control of your site rather than risk falling victim to deletion, however unlikely it

Building Your Web Presence

maybe. Also, hosting your own site looks much more professional. Which domain would you take more seriously; mybookisawesome.blogspot.com or mybookisawesome.com?

So, in order to set-up your web presence, you will first need to buy a domain name and then purchase hosting. I have tried several registrars over the years and none compare to Go Daddy.

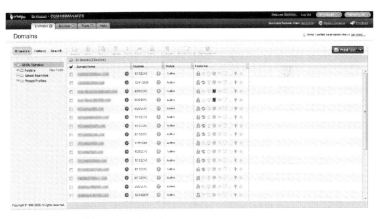

Fig. 4 - Go Daddy Domain Manager

Their service simply can not be beat. Sure, the shopping cart is a nightmare to navigate and really the Domain Manager (Fig. 4) isn't so great either, but, even considering all of that, they are still the best around. Their prices are low, their email support is responsive, and I have never once had a problem with a domain that I registered via their service. I wish that I could say the same for the other registrars, but unfortunately I simply can't.

Now that you have a domain, it's time to get hosting. I have tried many and can recommend only a few. From my experience the best around are as follows:

Fig. 5 – Fantastico

Reseller Zoom – This is my current web host. I started out using their Budget Reseller Hosting Plan, but due to the popularity of one of my blogs, I had to upgrade to one of their Failover Reseller Hosting Plans. They were very helpful during the whole process and always provide timely and helpful technical support.

Host Gator – This budget friendly web host also offers excellent support. I have called them a few times and have always been met with friendly, helpful, and courteous individuals. If you are just starting out, then their base-level hosting plan will be more than adequate and, best of all, it is extremely affordable.

Once you get your hosting account set-up and your domain has propagated, you can then either post your Blogger entries to your domain or install Wordpress. If your web host has Fantastico (Fig. 5) installed, which both of my recommended hosts do, then installing Wordpress will be easy. Just click a few buttons, fill-in a few pieces of information, and before you know it, you will have your own blog. With its default theme it will be a pretty drab, ordinary-looking blog, but it will be a blog nonetheless; and that's a start.

Make Your Theme Unique to You

In order to be taken seriously, you will need to have a professional-looking blog, so that default theme just isn't going to cut it. I really am an advocate of having a theme that sets you apart from all others and there are two ways to accomplish that. If you, or someone you know, has any knowledge about customizing themes, then get to work. Find a theme that you like and change it around until it looks unlike its former self.

If this free option simply isn't possible for you then you could investigate purchasing a premium theme. Sure, a few other people will be using that same theme, but the number of duplicates will be greatly reduced. Now, when you are just starting out, I don't recommend this option as the less money spent the better. That being said, this might be your only option for setting your blog apart from the rest if customizing a theme isn't possible for you.

Fig. 6 – Elegant Themes

POD Publicity

Fig. 7 – Premium Themes

There are a few places out there offering premium themes and, just like everything else, some are great and some are awful. Three premium theme sellers that I recommend are; Elegant Themes (Fig. 6), Premium Themes (Fig. 7), and ThemeForest (Fig 8). I have used themes from each, so I can attest to their quality.

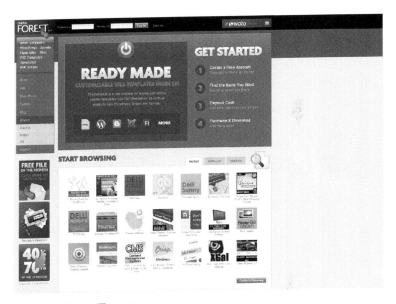

Fig. 8 – ThemeForest

The themes from Elegant Themes are much cheaper. As of this writing you could subscribe for one year for the very low price of only $19.95. That subscription grants you access to every Wordpress theme previously released by this designer as well as every theme released during your year as a subscriber.

Premium Themes differs in that you can either purchase a specific Wordpress theme or join The Premium Themes Club to access all of their themes. While they are more expensive, I still recommend them because their themes are of such high quality.

At ThemeForest thousands of designers submit their Wordpress and Blogger themes for sale. Themes are priced starting from five dollars, so you can easily find a bargain. Also, there are so many different designs to choose from that you are sure to find something that you like.

No matter which service you choose you are guaranteed to receive a quality theme that will give your blog a professional appearance.

Extra! Extra! Create an Online Media Kit All About It

You now have a blog, but that doesn't mean that you are ready to start writing blog posts just yet. First, there is a page on your blog that you will need to create. If you want to get publicity for your book, then the best thing that you can do is make things as easy as possible for journalists, reviewers, and interviewers.

The media is filled with very busy people, so the easier you make things the more likely you will be to receive publicity. You can do this by creating a comprehensive media kit and posting it online at your web site. Then, when you contact individuals about publicizing your book, you can tell them about your media kit and what it has to offer. Once you have shown them that your media kit contains every piece of information that they could possibly need to tell the world about your title, you can then provide them with its URL so that they can afford themselves of this helpful resource.

So, now that you know that you need an online media kit, you are probably wondering what it should contain. The following list contains some elements that will make for a phenomenal media kit. You don't have to include all of the listed items, and some of what you will include will depend upon whether your title is non-fiction or fiction. Just keep in mind that the more information that you provide the better your odds are of receiving publicity for your book.

Press Release – The media is filled with busy people and they will certainly look more favorably upon anyone who helps make their life easier. That is why a well-written press release is so important. The key is that your press release must be newsworthy. If it isn't then it will really do your promotion efforts more harm than good because you will create a poor first impression from which you may never recover.

Notable Reviews – If you have gotten your book reviewed by a well-known publication or web site, then let the media know by including it in your kit. There is a certain degree of "me too" when it comes to the media, so if they know that one of their peers loved your book, then they are much more likely to mention it as well. That is why it is so important to include favorable reviews from notable sources in your media kit.

Downloadable Cover Art – This is one element of your media kit that is absolutely vital. You should, without a doubt, include a low-resolution version of your book cover for online usage and a high-resolution version for print media.

Downloadable Author Photo – If you aren't the shy type, then you might also want to include both low and high-resolution images of yourself. People like to see the person behind the book and this will allow them to connect with you as the author.

Author Bio – As mentioned, the media and your readers want to connect with you as a person. That is where your author biography comes in since it allows you to tell the media all about you. To write your bio, simply provide a little background information about yourself. Also, if your book is non-fiction, be sure to include details on what qualifies you to write about your subject.

Customer Reviews – Once customer reviews start appearing at Amazon, you should include a sampling of the best ones in your media kit. Once the media sees that the public enjoys your book then they will be enticed to share your book with their readers since they will feel confident that they are providing them with a worthy recommendation.

Sample Content – The media loves excerpts and that is

why providing them with sample content is a must. Excerpts greatly increase your odds of garnering coverage for your book because the media simply eats them up. That is because sample content makes their job so much easier. An excerpt allows them to write only an opening paragraph and a closing paragraph with your content in between in order to generate quick content for their web site or publication.

Email Address – Sure, the media that you contact will already have your contact information, but what about people who find your media kit in other ways? Make sure to provide your email address in your media kit so that anyone who wants to publicize your book can contact you.

Pre-Written Blurbs – As was mentioned a few times previously, the media doesn't have a lot of time and they absolutely love it when you provide them with ready-made content. We have already covered the press release and sample content, but now let's address pre-written blurbs. If you provide short pre-written pieces that pertain to the subject matter of your book then you will find that many publications will use this ready-made content for filler. This is a win-win for both you and the media since they get quick and easy content and you get publicity for your book.

FAQs – A FAQs section is pretty much only applicable for non-fiction titles. After all, how many frequently asked questions can there be about a work of fiction? If yours is a work of non-fiction, however, you should include answers to questions that people might have about your book. These FAQs should also be provided on a page of their own, elsewhere on your site. That way causal visitors will also have ready access to them, since it is unlikely that they will be reading your media kit.

Chapter 4

Navigating the Amazon

Imagine if you had the opportunity to try and convince every visitor to your book's detail page that your title was the best choice. You could provide them with answers to questions that they might have, wow them with rave reviews that your book has received, tell them why you are qualified to write about this subject, and keep them up-to-date on happenings with your current and future titles. Who wouldn't jump at the chance to do all of that?

Well, Amazon offers authors the chance to do just that, but, oddly, many authors don't afford themselves of this opportunity. Perhaps it is because

POD Publicity

they don't know that Amazon offers these tools or they think that it would be too much trouble to bother with. Their loss, however, is your gain, because by utilizing the tools that Amazon provides, you can set yourself and your book apart as you make your mark in the marketplace.

Fig. 9 – Book Content Update Form

Pimp Your Book Detail Page

After your book is listed at Amazon, your first stop should be to visit the Book Content Update Form (Fig. 9). When you arrive at this page, you will be asked to provide contact information and your book's ISBN. Once that data has been submitted, you will then arrive at the second page where you can enhance your book's detail page. Here you will find fields to submit the following information.

- Description
- Publisher's comments
- Author comments
- Author bio(s)
- Table of contents
- Inside flap copy
- Back cover copy
- Reviews
- Excerpt

Be sure to complete the form as fully as possible. Remember that the more information you provide the better your book's detail page will look in comparison with those of other titles. That will, in turn, make your book that much more attractive to buyers.

Happily, completing this form will be an easy task. Much of the information that is asked for here is already available in your media kit. That means that you can simply copy and paste the required information.

This form is so simple to complete that I really only need to address one field and that is the one for reviews. If you don't have any reviews at this time, then that is fine. Complete as much of the form as possible and then revisit it once your book has received reviews. Once you do have reviews, extract the best excerpt from each of them and enter it here. These review excerpts will be posted on your book's detail page and act as testimonials for your title. As you continue to garner publicity for your book, you will need to revisit this page often so that you can enter the latest glowing recommendations.

Author Central

Now for the part where you claim your book and Amazon allows you to communicate with your customers. First off, you are going to need an Amazon account to be able to participate in Author Central (Fig. 10).

Formerly, when this feature was called AmazonConnect, it was highly advisable to create a separate account for use with the service. The reason for this was that, with AmazonConnect, if you used your personal account, your author profile page would contain any customer information associated with that account such as reviews, purchase activity, wish lists, registries, etc. Now, some of this information could be hidden, but some of it could not. For that reason, it was especially important to just start fresh with a new account that didn't have any history attached to it.

With Author Central, however, Amazon says that this information will be kept private. The choice is yours as to whether you use your current account or start fresh. Personally, I would still recommend creating a new account that can be used solely in association with Author Central. That way, should there be any glitches in the system, your private customer information will never be shared with your readers.

If you elect to create a new account, then you should know that some of the Amazon-related promotional techniques mentioned in this book will not be available to you until Amazon considers your account to be valid and verified. To meet this requirement you must make a purchase from your new account using an approved credit or debit card. All things considered, this really isn't that much trouble to go to in order to ensure that your information is kept private.

Navigating the Amazon

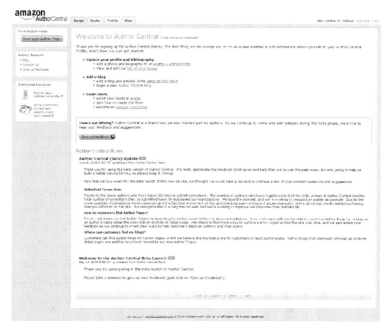

Fig. 10 – Author Central

Now that we have that out of the way, let's get you set up with Author Central. First, either sign-in or sign-up. Once that is finished, you will need to search for any books that you have written so that they can be added to your bibliography. First, click on the **Books** tab at the top of the screen. You may find that your titles have already been added to your Author Central account. If that is the case, then you can move on. If, however, one or more of your titles are missing, click on the button labeled **Add more books**. In the search box, type your name. Once you locate your title, you can then click the button located underneath the book that is labeled **This is my book**. If Amazon's catalog lists your name as the author, then you are all done. You shouldn't have to wait more than 3 days for a newly added title to appear in your bibliography.

Amazon uses your account information to verify you as an author. If they cannot verify you based on that information, then Amazon will have to contact one of your publishers for verification. If verification is required, then the length of time before your book appears in your bibliography may be longer.

You may find that the information associated with one of your titles is incorrect. If that is the case, then click on the book shown on your books page and select the link entitled **Suggest product information updates**. From that page you will be able to update any erroneous information that has been associated with your book. Now that you have claimed your books and ensured that all information associated with them is correct, you should begin work on your author profile page.

First up is your photo. Once again, if you aren't the shy type, then you should upload a photo to your profile page. Readers like to connect with the author and including a photo is an excellent way for them to do that. Next, you can enter your biography. Since you already wrote a bio to include in your online media kit, you can easily paste it here.

On the homepage for your Author Central account you will see that you can import an RSS feed for a blog that you already write or that you can create a new Author Central blog. I strongly advise against the first option. Do not, under any circumstances, post content here that you also post to your own blog. Doing so would create duplicate content and dilute the effectiveness of your main blog. If people can read your

POD Publicity

posts at Amazon then why would they ever visit your site? Also, duplicating your content on Amazon could have an adverse effect on your blog's rankings in the search engines.

I will now briefly mention some of the other features that you will find in Author Central. In your account you will find a link that you can click to enroll your books in the Kindle program. That link will be of importance when you read Chapter 7 where we discuss the benefits of selling your book in many formats. On your Author Central homepage you will also see a link that allows you to join Search Inside the Book. If you are a CreateSpace user, then your book is entered in the program by default. For other publishers, however, this link will be particularly useful.

Fig. 11 – Tags

Tags

Next up, you will need to visit your book detail page. There you will scroll down until you see the section devoted to product tags (Fig. 11). It is important that you are the first person to tag your book with appropriate keywords. The reason for this is that you will then be permanently associated with each keyword that appears on your book detail page. You may have noticed that I said "appropriate keywords." It is very important that you only enter keywords that are actually associated with your work. If you attempt to spam the system then you will instantly lose credibility with your readers and, most probably, subject yourself to punishment from Amazon.

Amazon's tagging system comes in handy for directing people to your title. Suppose that someone is viewing a book similar to yours. When they scroll down the book detail page for that title, they may encounter a tag and click it. If you associated that tag with your product, then your book will be shown to that potential buyer.

Tag for Amazon Search

This may seem confusing considering that we just covered tags, but in this section we will now examine a totally different kind of tag at Amazon. On your book detail page there is a section that encourages people to help others find the product on that particular page. They can do this by tagging the product for search. What this basically means is that people can submit keywords that are relevant to a book and Amazon will show that item in Amazon search results when people perform a search for that word or phrase.

As part of your efforts to sell books, you should make sure to tag your own book for search. Doing so will make your book that much more visible to customers. When undertaking this process, don't expect instant results. Amazon estimates that suggestions will appear on the site within two weeks. Also, each person is only permitted to submit ten search suggestions per product, so consider your tags carefully before submitting.

Listmania!

This feature provides you with the opportunity to create a list of product recommendations based on a particular subject. These are especially beneficial because Listmania! (Fig. 12) lists appear on both search results pages and book detail pages. You may be tempted to include very few items on your list, but you should add at least 10 products in order to make the list beneficial to shoppers.

Brainstorm a few lists that you could create along with catchy titles to go along with them. For example, good titles would include:

- *Top 10 Books for Quick and Easy Crafts*
- *Sci-Fi Stories That Are Out of This World*
- *20 Titles That Will Help You Become a Better Writer*

If you create titles similar to the aforementioned then you will be sure to generate clicks on your Listmania! lists.

When creating your Listmania! list, you will see an area where you can add a few words about your qualifications. This is where you tell people why you are suited to recommend these products.

Next, you should write an introduction for your list. This doesn't need to be long and elaborate. It should simply tell people what your list is about. While you are certainly creating this list in order to promote your book, that shouldn't be what you tell people. In the introduction you should make the purpose of the list about the reader. Tell them how reading your recommendations will make things better for them.

Fig. 12 – Listmania!

Tags should be entered next. They will help people locate your Listmania! list and the more opportunity that people have to find it the better. Be sure to add only relevant tags rather than resorting to keyword stuffing.

Click the **Add a product** button and, in the pop-up box, search for products that would be well-suited to the theme of the list. You may think it best to be modest and avoid placing your book in the top spot on the list. Well, modesty doesn't have any place when you are trying to sell books, so go ahead and put your book in the top spot. You may feel compelled to disclose that you wrote the book in the top spot, but I don't really feel that this is required.

As you are adding products to your list you will also be prompted to add comments. While this is not required, I do recommend it. Be sure that the comments for all of the products on your list are positive and professional.

You may be tempted to create many, many Listmania! lists, but it is important that you avoid that temptation as it will do much to tarnish your credibility as you will look like a spammer in the eyes of just about everyone. Instead, only create viable Listmania! lists that can be viewed as beneficial.

So You'd Like to...Guides

The more effort required for any given promotional

technique the less likely people will be to take advantage of its benefits. Creating a So You'd Like to...Guide (Fig. 13) involves a certain amount of effort, which means that most people won't bother with them. That also means that, if you invest the time to create one, it will have less competition, which is exactly why you should take advantage of this promotional technique.

You can access the link to create a So You'd Like to...Guide from your profile page. Once you click on the link you will see a field were you can enter the name of your guide. In order to do this, you will need to finish the sentence So You'd Like to...

Once you have settled on a title, you will need to enter your qualifications. It is important that you maintain consistency, so just enter the same thing here that you entered when creating your Listmania! List. Now, it's time to enter some tags. Remember to keep these relevant to the subject of your guide.

Fig. 13 – So You'd Like to...

So, you are probably thinking that this seems pretty easy and wondering how I could possibly say that the process requires a certain amount of effort. Well, you are about to find out. In the last section of the page you will need to write the guide itself, which must consist of at least 100 words and at most 5,000 words.

Basically, you will need to enter a product using the instructions provided on the guide creation page and then write something about it that is applicable to the topic of your guide.

A So You'd Like to...Guide wouldn't be much use to you if it didn't help you sell books, so be sure to mention your own product within the guide. Amazon states in their guide instructions, "Up to the first three products you mention will be featured at the top of your guide..." So, don't mention your book just anywhere in your guide. Grab your book a featured spot by mentioning it first thing.

Once your guide is finished and saved, Amazon will begin displaying it randomly on relevant book detail pages. Relevancy is determined by the products that you choose to mention in your guide, so think carefully when deciding which products to include as you will only want to mention products within your book's subject area.

Amapedia

Amapedia is an Amazon-run product wiki where anyone can write or modify content. Amapedia entries are characterized by the fact that they must contain only factual information, which means that you will need to keep your opinions to yourself. As a user, you should post entries in your field of expertise. Now, who has more expert knowledge on your book than you? Every little bit of exposure helps, so head on over to Amapedia and write an entry for your book.

Buy X, Get Y

If you aren't familiar with Amazon's Buy X, Get Y (BXGY) program, then allow me to give you a brief overview. With this program, designed for small publishers, you pay a fee to have your book paired with another book for a predetermined amount of time. During that period of time, customers can purchase both titles at a discount.

Now, from that description the program probably sounds great and you are likely wondering where you go to sign-up. Yes, if your book is paired with a popular title, BXGY will increase your book's exposure, but the more popular the title that you choose to be paired with, the more money you will need to spend. Fees for the BXGY program can easily cost $1000 a month. Spending that fee would saddle you with debt and put you that much farther away from your goal of realizing a profit from your book sales. Do you realize just how many books that you would need to sell in order to make that money back?

Your goal in this endeavor is to generate profit not saddle yourself with massive debt. It is for this reason that I cannot recommend the BXGY program to print-on-demand publishers. Perhaps, after you are generating considerable profit from your title, you might want to revisit the program and see if participation seems wise at that time. Until then, however, give this one a pass and focus on other avenues that are just as effective and a whole lot cheaper.

Customer Image Gallery

In your effort to bombard potential buyers with incentives to buy your title, there is one feature that should not be overlooked. That is the Customer Image Gallery. Here Amazon allows customers to upload images that are relevant to your book. So, not only can you use your book detail page to verbally appeal to your audience, you can also appeal to them visually. This feature is of little use to fiction authors, but for non-fiction writers it is invaluable. Even if your book doesn't lend itself to photos, you can still take advantage of this feature. Perhaps you have diagrams in your book. Why not upload a few to pique interest?

Customer Communities

Amazon encourages discussion amongst its customers and, if you are serious about selling books, then you really should join in. It is not possible to include a signature file at the bottom of every post, but participation includes other benefits. As you participate in the community do your best to be helpful and to establish yourself as an expert in your book's subject area. As you gain credibility you will also gain customers.

One important thing that you should keep in mind as you post is never try to sell your book. Nothing will turn people off faster than a sales pitch. Also, steel yourself to the fact that you are going to run into some nasty people. That is just a fact of discussion forums. In situations such as these, you must remain professional and always take the high road. Your reputation is, after all, at stake, so getting into a petty argument really isn't worth destroying the credibility that you have worked so hard to establish.

Now you may be wondering how the members of the community will even learn about your book if you aren't able to include a signature and you shouldn't mention it in your posts. The answer to that is easy. Your name will be linked, and anyone who is interested in learning more about you can click on it to view your profile page. If you are a truly helpful and friendly member of the community then others will certainly become intrigued and want to learn more about you. It is then that your profile page can work its magic to sell your book.

Writing Reviews

Writing reviews on Amazon for other products is a great way to gain exposure for your book. That being said, please, please do not go overboard with it. Only review products that you have actually purchased and do not make the review a sales pitch for your book. As a matter of fact, Amazon now specifically prohibits this.

Even though you can't mention your own book in the review, this technique will still be beneficial because it will allow you to garner exposure since each review that you write is linked to your profile page where people can learn all about your title.

How to Deal with Negative Reviews

If you are lucky, you will never have to deal with receiving a negative review at Amazon. In the event that you should receive a negative review, however, know that all is not lost. It is possible to have that review removed. That isn't to say that you should contest every one or two star review, but if you find that a review is completely unfounded, then don't hesitate to try to have it taken down. What you will need to do is contact Amazon at **community-help@amazon.com** and present your case. If, after reviewing the matter, they find that the review does not meet their guidelines, then they will remove it within a few days.

Chapter 5

Getting the Publicity Machine Up and Running

This chapter begins by my telling you to do as I say and not as I did. When I was soliciting publicity, I opted to send each and every contact a hard copy of my book. If I had it to do over again, I wouldn't have done this. There is a very good reason for my change of heart. See, when I contacted people and asked them to inspect my book, a lot of people said yes. The problem is, however, that after I sent them the book, a lot of those people didn't follow through and write a review, article, or anything else.

So, if I had it to do over again, I would not send

hard copies and you shouldn't either. Whenever possible, opt to send an ebook. That way you won't be out any money if they don't follow through.

The Reviewer Package in Review

You may, for whatever reason, prefer to send out hard copies of your book rather than emailing ebooks. If that is the case, then you will have to put together a reviewer package that should include a book, a review slip, and a cover letter. Let's examine each of these in more detail.

Book – You may be tempted to send a damaged edition, but that is not advisable. Always send a pristine copy of your book as this will make a much better first impression.

Resales will hurt your bottom line, so you should do what you can to prevent them. One step that you can take is to deter recipients from reselling your book.

This can be done by using a rubber stamp to mark each and every review copy that you send out. Use the stamp to mark one edge of the book. That way the fact that this is a review copy is clearly visible upon first inspection.

Review Slip – The purpose of the review slip (Fig. 14) is to provide vital information that will be needed when writing about your book. A piece of paper can easily get lost or misplaced, so simply adding the review slip to the envelope along with your other materials is not the best course of action. Instead, you should use a glue stick to affix the review slip to either the inside front cover or the title page of your book.

You will notice that, in addition to the vital information, the slip also directs contacts to visit the online media kit for your book. This is beneficial because it saves you money that would otherwise have to be spent were you to include a press release and samples reviews in your reviewer package. It is also beneficial because it allows these individuals to easily afford themselves of all the helpful resources that you have placed at their disposal.

Lewis Carroll presents *The Wonderful Wizard of Oz* for your consideration

Title: *The Wonderful Wizard of Oz*
Author: Lewis Carroll
Edition: First
ISBN-10: 1234567812 **ISBN-13:** 1234567812345
Pages: 225
Price: $16.95
Publication date: January 22, 1900
Rights: Permission is granted to reprint brief excerpts and quotations from this book in reviews and articles.
Media Kit: A press release, cover image, author bio, and more can be found at: http://ozbookurl.com

It would be appreciated if you would send a copy of your review to: **lcarroll@ozbookurl.com**

Fig. 14 – Book review slip

Cover Letter – Think of the cover letter as a reintroduction. A reviewer package, after all, isn't much good if the receipt doesn't remember why they are receiving it. So, use your cover letter to briefly remind the recipient of your previous communication about publicity for your book.

You might opt to end your letter after providing a reminder or you may feel the need to include additional content. It is just important to remember that the cover letter should be as concise as possible.

Lastly, when preparing your reviewer packages for shipment, be sure to include adequate packing material to ensure that the materials arrive in good condition. After all, there would be no point in sending a pristine edition of your book only to allow it to become damaged during shipping.

Publicity Seekers Can Be Choosers

When I was soliciting publicity for my print-on-demand titles, I had certain criteria that potential contacts must meet in order to make it worth my while to reach out to them. There is no point, after all, in wasting your efforts by contacting someone who can't improve your odds of selling books. These criteria will be addressed shortly, but let us first begin by talking about where to begin your search for contacts. As with most things, your search should begin with Google. Here are some searches that I suggest you run.

> *your keyword book review*
> *your keyword blog*
> *book reviews*
> *your keyword magazine*

Those keyword searches should yield good results, but there is one search that you can run that should produce an avalanche of results. This keyword search is an excellent way for you to use your competition to your advantage.

First, you will need to compile a small list of titles that your book is competing with. Once you have done that, return to Google and enter the following search string:

competitor's book title review

The results that appear after performing this search will be filled with sites that have written a review for your competition. That means that these people have shown a willingness to write reviews about books in your niche. As such, they should be more than willing to provide a review for your book as well.

If you can think of more keyword searches to run, then by all means do. Those are just some suggested keyword combinations that are guaranteed to produce results.

After you have exhausted Google, it is then time to move on to other sites to conduct more searches. Your next stop should be the Technorati Top 100 (Fig. 15). You will need to visit every page to see if there are any sites that either have a book review section or match the topic of your book.

Next up, you are going to want to find some newspapers to contact. At this point your main focus should be newspapers in your area. You will be contacting a couple national papers, but for the most part, at this time, it is best to focus on your own local area. Once the publicity machine starts rolling and you begin to get press then you can begin contacting newspapers across your country and the world. So, to find all of the newspapers in your local area you should pay a visit to RefDesk. There you will find a comprehensive list of newspapers by state and, also, worldwide. In addition to local papers, you should also add *USA Today* and *The New York Times* to your list.

As was mentioned, all of the sites that you find

are not going to be worth contacting to request publicity. So, how do you know when to make contact and when to just close the browser window and move on? You can determine which contacts are worthwhile by using the following checklist.

Fig. 15 – Technorati Top 100

POD Publicity

Fig. 16 – Alexa

Alexa Rating – Okay, let's be realistic. Alexa (Fig. 16) ratings are notoriously inaccurate but these numbers can be considered as long as you evaluate additional sources as well. It was my practice, when promoting, to largely avoid soliciting publicity from sites with an Alexa rating higher than 500,000. My reason for this was that I didn't want to waste the time and effort on sites with low readerships as any publicity that they might offer would do very little to produce sales.

Quantcast – This site is a dream for print-on-demand authors looking to promote their work. It provides not only traffic statistics but demographic information about a site's audience as well. Head on over to Quantcast (Fig. 17) and look at the numbers for each site that you are considering contacting. Once again, if their rank is below 500,000, then great. The site looks like a keeper. Before you commit to anything, however, next review their demographics. If you have a good idea about who your book will appeal to, and you should, you will then easily be able to determine if their audience matches that of your book. If you find that the site's demographics are vastly different from your book's, then it's best to move on to investigating other sites for possible publicity.

If you try to research a site at Quantcast and they aren't listed that doesn't necessarily mean that you should cross them off of your list. This service isn't infallible and some very big sites haven't been

POD Publicity

Quantified. In instances such as these you will just have to evaluate the other information that you have been able to gather about the site and ultimately make a judgment call in order to decide if they seem worthwhile.

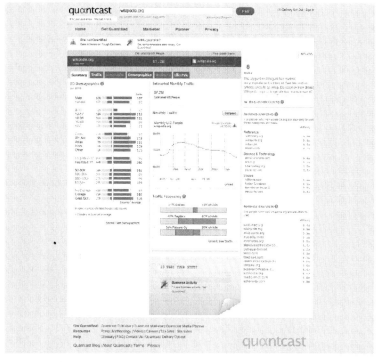

Fig. 17 – Quantcast

Feedburner Subscribers – A lot of bloggers include a Feedburner FeedCount Chicklet on their site that displays the number of subscribers to their RSS feed. This will provide you with invaluable information about the size of their audience. The higher the number displayed on the chicklet the more people you will be able to reach should that blogger choose to publicize your book. If you find that their chicklet displays a number below 300, then the audience for that blog really isn't large enough to be beneficial.

Circulation – This is obviously only going to apply to magazines and newspapers. Visit Wikipedia and search for any newspapers or magazines that you are considering contacting for publicity. On the wiki page, you will find the publication's daily circulation. If that number is less than 10,000, then pass on that publication and move on to investigating the next.

Publicity Is a Numbers Game

During this process, you are going to need to find hundreds of potential sources for publicity, because the sad fact is that most of the people that you contact will either ignore you or say no to your request. This is a case where the law of large numbers really does apply. The more people that you ask for publicity the more likely you are to get a sufficient number of positive replies. As you begin the promotion process, you should aim for 100 positive responses. To achieve that response rate, you will probably need to contact about 500 people.

That may seem like a lot, but it isn't as bad as it sounds. If you can contact 500 people and get 100 yeses then you will have a positive response rate of 20%, which is quite good.

What to Do When You've Found a Keeper

During the process of locating potential contacts, you are going to be gathering a lot of information. When you find a contact that passes the checklist requirements then you are going to need to keep track of the details of their site as this information will come in handy later.

I can tell you from experience that, during this process, a spreadsheet is going to be your best friend. In your spreadsheet you will enter some of the information that you gather during the search process as well as many other additional details.

Let's add an entry to give you an idea of how the process works. Suppose that I am writing a book about knitting and I want to contact the Knitting Guide at About.com for a review. After conducting my initial research, my spreadsheet started-off looking like the one shown in Figure 18.

Site Name	Site URL	Alexa Rating	Quantcast Rank	Feedburner Subscribers	Circulation
About.com: Kntting	knitting.about.com	75	8146	Information unavailable	n/a

Fig. 18 – Review contact spreadsheet

Now, search the web site to find a contact name and a method of contact. Then, enter both into your spreadsheet as well (Fig 19).

Contact Name	Contact Method	Contacted?	Agreeable to receiving a review copy?	Review copy sent on	Publicity posted on
Sarah E. White	http://knitting.about.com/mpremail.htm	YES on 3/24	YES	03/30/09	04/14/09

Fig. 19 – Review contact spreadsheet (cont.)

Now, let's discuss a few of the other entries that appear in the example spreadsheet.

Contacted? - This field will allow you to enter if and when you made contact. This will allow you to avoid the embarrassment of accidentally emailing the same person twice to ask for publicity. It will also allow you to track when you first made contact. This is important to document because you will want to know when enough time has elapsed to follow-up if you don't hear back. If you don't receive a reply to your initial email after two weeks, then send along another message in order to check in. After I sent my first message to a handful of contacts, I didn't hear back, so I sent follow-up messages. Those follow-ups resulted in replies and, ultimately, publicity for my book.

Agreeable to receiving a review copy? - By tracking who said yes and who said no to receiving a review copy you will be able to easily see what percentage of your publicity efforts have been favorable.

Review copy sent on – The information entered here is also beneficial when it comes to following up. If a contact hasn't provided publicity for your book after two weeks, then send along a friendly message to ask if the review copy reached them successfully. You might just find that your book never arrived.

Publicity posted on – Here you will enter the date when the piece about your book was posted online or, in the case of print publications, the date on which it appeared in print. This information will allow you to track contacts who have done as promised and those who have failed to follow through.

First Contact

Now that you have collected a list of potential contacts, it is time to solicit some publicity. Your aim in this initial message is to tell the recipient who you are, what your book is about, and, finally, to ask for publicity in some form.

Allow them to decide what form that publicity should take. Perhaps the recipient isn't in the habit of posting reviews but they love interviews. Either way, let them know that, whatever the coverage, you would be happy to receive it.

In your first message, you must be sure to direct them to your online media kit and, lastly, offer to send them a review copy. It is important that you do not send them an ebook review copy when you first make contact since most people don't like to receive unsolicited attachments.

The following is a sample email to illustrate how you should go about making first contact. For the purposes of this example, let's say that you are Lewis Carroll trying to generate publicity for *The Wonderful Wizard of Oz*.

```
Hi (insert name),
```

```
    My name is Lewis Carroll. I have just
completed writing my latest book called The
Wonderful Wizard of Oz, and I was wondering
if you would like to receive a free review
copy.
```

The Wonderful Wizard of Oz tells the story of Dorothy as she travels over the rainbow to the Land of Oz. During her journey down the yellow brick road our heroine encounters an interesting cast of characters that includes the Scarecrow, the Tin Woodsman, the Cowardly Lion, as well as both the Good Witch of the North and The Wicked Witch of the West. Oh, and let's not forget about the flying monkeys.

If you enjoy your review copy, then I hope that you will be open to discussing possibilities for presenting this title to your audience. A book review, an article, an interview, or some combination of the aforementioned would be fantastic. Also, if you have positive comments, then I would certainly appreciate your taking the time to post a review at Amazon.com.

Please visit my web site (your URL here) where you will find my media kit which contains a wealth of information.

If you would like to receive a review copy, then please let me know and I will

```
send you an ebook as an email attachment.

Sincerely,

Lewis Carroll
```

Take note, in the third paragraph, how a mention is made to their posting an Amazon review. This is done in a very specific way in order to avoid bad reviews. You do not want to specifically ask for a good review at Amazon, but you can certainly suggest it. The wording in that sentence does just that. By saying, "if you have favorable comments" you are letting them know that if they don't have anything nice to say, then please don't say anything at all.

You will also notice that reference is made to sending an ebook as an attachment. This example, along with those that follow in the remainder of this text, are written as though you have opted to send review copies as ebooks. If you are planning to send hard copies of your book, however, then you will need to customize that paragraph to your own needs.

Please note that this email should only be used as an example on which you base your own first contact message. You should avoid the temptation to copy it word-for-word as that will only serve to dilute its effectiveness.

Hi, Remember Me?

When you are trying to drum up publicity for your book, writing follow-up messages is vital. People might get busy and forget about your previous communication or they might not take you seriously the first time that you contact them. Yes, sometimes they will just think that your message is spam. As I previously mentioned, you should follow-up with anyone that does not reply to your first message within two weeks.

In your follow-up message you should remind them of your first message and let them know that you are checking in to gauge their interest. You want to seem friendly and curious without appearing to be at all pushy. The following message would make for a nice follow-up. Once again, please remember to rewrite this sample email in your own words.

```
Hello again (name),

    A couple of weeks ago I emailed you to
ask if you would be interested in receiving
a review copy of my book The Wonderful
Wizard of Oz. I was curious if you have had
time to consider my offer. Please send me a
reply at your earliest convenience and let
me know if you would like to receive a free
review copy via email.

Sincerely,

Lewis Carroll
```

At this point I can't really offer additional example messages for this part of the exchange because the content of your correspondence will depend upon the responses that you receive. I can, however, offer some suggestions.

If you get a reply stating that they aren't interested, then write a short reply to simply thank them for their time. This will do wonders to make you look professional as you will show your willingness to thank them even though they have opted against publicizing your book.

If you get a favorable reply stating that they would like to publicize your book, then tell them that you are looking forward to reading the coverage and ask them when you can expect to see it published. That will set a deadline of sorts. If they fail to post anything by that date, then contact them once again and ask about the status of things.

The key to much of this process is following up. People need to be reminded and it is your job to do that in the friendliest way possible.

After they have posted something about your site then you will once again need to send along a message. Simply tell them that you enjoyed reading whatever it is that they posted and thank them for all that they have done to publicize your book.

When POD Publishers and Podcasters Unite

Podcasts are really no different than radio shows except for the fact that they are delivered online. Being interviewed by a podcaster can do wonders for your publicity push because it will expose your book to hundreds or thousands of listeners.

In order to locate podcasts suitable for promoting your book you will once again need to begin with Google. Once there, I would suggest that you enter the following search term:

your keyword podcast

After you have exhausted that search, launch iTunes where you will run the same search. After that, you will have one last stop, which is Podcast Pickle, where you can search for podcasts by genre.

In order to keep track of things, you should create another spreadsheet (Fig. 20) like the one that you previously created. This time, however, you will want to customize the fields so that they are appropriate to the situation. For example, your new spreadsheet should resemble the one shown below.

Podcast Name	Site URL	Contact Name	Contact Method	Contacted?	Agreeable to an interview?

Fig. 20 - Podcaster contact spreadsheet

When contacting podcasters to request an interview, your email will look similar to the one that you previously sent to bloggers, magazines, and newspapers. Here is a sample for you to work from. Remember to change things up while retaining the overall message of the email since sending this exact message will destroy its effectiveness.

Hi (insert name),

My name is Lewis Carroll. I have just completed writing my latest book called *The Wonderful Wizard of Oz*, and I was wondering if you would like to receive a free review copy.

The Wonderful Wizard of Oz tells the story of Dorothy as she travels over the rainbow to the Land of Oz. During her journey down the yellow brick road our heroine encounters an interesting cast of characters that includes the Scarecrow, the Tin Woodsman, the Cowardly Lion, as well as both the Good Witch of the North, and The Wicked Witch of the West. Oh, and let's not forget about the flying monkeys.

If you enjoy your review copy, then I hope that you will be open to discussing the possibility of presenting this title to your audience. In my opinion, a book review or an interview would be ideal ways to do that, but I am certainly open to any suggestions that you might have.

Please visit my web site (your URL here) where you will find my media kit which contains a wealth of information.

If you would like to receive a review copy, then please let me know and I will send you an ebook as an email attachment.

Sincerely,

Lewis Carroll

Today's Very Special Guest Blogger Is...You

Writing a post for a well-known blog is an excellent way to get the word out about your book. Guest blogging is great because it basically acts as an endorsement from the host blog that tells their readers that you are an expert in your field. That will make your efforts to sell your book to their audience even more effective.

So, you are probably wondering how to go about getting a blogger to allow you to act as a guest blogger. Well, here is where your spreadsheet will come in handy once again. Visit each site in your spreadsheet to see if they have information posted about guest blogging opportunities. If not, then you should contact them again about the possibility of writing a guest post. Remind them of your previous communication just so that they remember who you are. Next, ask if they use guest bloggers and tell them that you would be happy to provide a post if they are agreeable. If they reply favorably, then you are all set and just need to write-up a winning post that will wow both the blogger and their readers.

Amazon Reviewers

People who have written a review on Amazon have already shown a willingness to share their opinions with buyers. You can use this fact to your advantage by asking them if they would be open to posting a review about your book.

While you should be open to contacting all suitable Amazon reviewers, keep in mind, during your search, that a special effort should be made to contact Top Reviewers. People who post enough reviews at Amazon are rewarded with Top Reviewer status. It is kind of like Amazon's way of saying that these reviewers really know their stuff, so getting one of them to review your book can really pay off.

To begin, you will need to search for products similar to your book. If you can find reviewers who have previously reviewed products in your niche then that pre-qualifies them as being interested in your subject area.

When you locate someone who seems like they would be suitable, click on their name. Once you arrive at their profile page be sure to read it throughly. Some reviewers provide information to review seekers telling them just what sort of products they will or will not consider reviewing. If you determine that a reviewer is a good match for your book, then look to see if they have provided a contact method, as some reviewers post an email address or postal address in their profile.

If you are unable to locate a method of contact, then all is not lost. You can still submit your review request by clicking the link labeled **Invite to be an Amazon Friend.** Doing this will allow you to enter a message that will be sent through Amazon's system to your selected recipient.

The message that you send to an Amazon reviewer should be carefully crafted so that you don't sound at all pushy. As matter of fact, you can really just get by with tweaking the message that you have been using all along to generate publicity. Once again, here is a sample for you to put in your own words.

POD Publicity

Hi (insert name),

My name is Lewis Carroll. I was searching for reviewers with an interest in (insert genre here) when I located you. I have just completed writing my latest book called *The Wonderful Wizard of Oz*, and I was wondering if you would like to receive a free review copy.

The Wonderful Wizard of Oz tells the story of Dorothy as she travels over the rainbow to the Land of Oz. During her journey down the yellow brick road our heroine encounters an interesting cast of characters that includes the Scarecrow, the Tin Woodsman, the Cowardly Lion, as well as both the Good Witch of the North, and The Wicked Witch of the West. Oh, and let's not forget about the flying monkeys.

If you enjoy your review copy, then I would hope that you would be open to sharing your review of it at Amazon.com.

If you would like to receive a review copy, then please let me know and I will send you an ebook as an email attachment.

Sincerely,

Lewis Carroll

Once again, you are going to have to send a lot of messages in order to get a satisfactory number of positive responses. Just keep at it and you will see positive results. Don't be offended if you don't receive a response to your message. There could be a million reasons why you won't hear back. For example, some Amazon Top Reviewers get a lot of review requests so they may just not have the time to get back to you. If you don't receive a reply then, in this situation, it's best not to follow-up. Just take the lack of response in stride and move on to the next step in your publicity efforts.

Distributing a Press Release Isn't so Pressing

A lot of people probably aren't going to agree with

what I am about to tell you, but here goes. Distributing a press release is pretty much going to be a waste of your time. I'm not saying that a press release is pointless. If you read the chapter on putting together an online media kit then you will see that I did advise you to include a press release. I'm just saying that you shouldn't take the time to mass distribute it. A press release will be much more effective and generate more publicity sitting right there in your media kit than it ever will should you use a service to distribute it.

The reason for this being that the reporters who receive press releases via mass distribution will, most likely, not give them much attention unless they are really wowed by them. Some won't be in your target audience, others will be too busy to give your press release their full attention, and a few will just have more important news to report. Whatever the reason, mass distribution will result in limited success. The people that you email and direct to your online media kit, however, will be much more targeted to your message since you took the time to handpick each and every one of them.

So, as you can see, I'm not advising against using a press release. I'm just telling you the best way to use it so that the time that you spend promoting your book is used most effectively.

Article Marketing

It really is amazing just how much can be accomplished with just one article. Each article that you write and distribute will perform a variety of purposes, all of which will do wonders to improve your odds of selling books. Just imagine what you could achieve with 50, 100, or more articles; all out there on the Internet working for you. Here are just a few of the benefits that you can expect as a result of article marketing.

Web Site Visitors – By including the URL to your web site in your resource box, the articles that you have written will draw visitors into your site. The more popular the site that reprints your article, the more visitors that you can expect to receive. This is beneficial because, once those visitors arrive at your site, you will then have a chance to convert them from visitor to buyer.

Link Popularity – Most search engines believe that sites with several incoming links are of greater importance and they typically reward these sites with a higher ranking in the search results. By distributing articles with a link to your site in the resource box you will be able to generate more incoming links and increase your site's ranking in the search engines which will mean a greater number of searchers will find your site.

Expert Status – If you provide valuable information in your articles then people will soon come to respect and trust you. When that happens, you will find that you have established yourself as an expert in your field. Once you have reached expert status, selling books will become that much easier.

Now that you have seen some of the benefits of article marketing, I think that this would be a good time for a word of caution. You may be tempted to recycle content from your blog and submit those posts to the article repositories. If you do this then you won't be doing yourself or your web site any favors. It is still not confirmed if there actually is a duplicate content penalty, but do you really want to take the chance and find out that the speculation is true? In book promotion, corners can't be cut and this is one instance where that couldn't be more true. Take the time to write original content and you will feel safe in knowing that this promotional technique isn't jeopardizing your web site in any way.

To take advantage of this promotional technique you will need to write informative, helpful articles and then submit them to a select number of article repositories. You may have noticed that I said "a select number" and there was a reason for that. You could waste hours submitting your articles to every repository under the sun, but doing that won't accomplish much. Instead, you should only focus your efforts on submitting articles to the most popular and highly-trafficked repositories.

There is also another reason why it is best to limit your article submission efforts to a select number of repositories. Submitting your article to every imaginable repository may actually make you look like a spammer in the eyes of the search engines. If that should occur then your article marketing efforts would wind up hurting rather than helping your web site ranking.

With all of that in mind, you should focus your article marketing efforts on only the following sites:

- **EzineArticles**
- **GoArticles**
- **IdeaMarketers**

If you make a concerted effort to submit content to those sites then you will, over time, be rewarded for your efforts.

Chapter 6

Networking Works

How much more likely would you be to go see a movie if you knew someone in the film? The odds are pretty good that you would be there opening day. Your motivation might be to help your acquaintance have impressive opening day ticket sales or you might just be curious how they did in the film.

Those are the benefits of networking. In the aforementioned scenario your fictional friend will have sold a ticket just because they made the effort to get to know you. Hopefully that example will have shown you how valuable networking can be. Networking brings all sorts of benefits from growing a customer-base to building relationships with your peers. There are many ways that you can go about networking, so let's examine each technique.

Carry on a Conversation

When you were configuring your blog, you may have wondered if you should allow readers to post comments. If you turned off the comments feature, then I am here to tell you to go turn it back on. Allowing visitors to your site the option of posting comments does wonders for letting them feel as though you aren't just a name on a book cover, but an actual person.

To truly accomplish this feat, however, you must interact with them. After all, no one likes having a one-sided conversation. When they post comments, write replies. If their comment includes a question, then do your best to provide the answer. Do everything that you can to endear yourself to them and create a sense of community.

Allowing comments and interacting with your readers will do wonders to encourage them to return to your site and, once they like and respect you, they will be more likely to want to read your work.

Now, a word of warning. The sad fact is that allowing comments opens your blog up to being abused by spammers. If you are using Wordpress, then you can combat these comment spammers by installing a plugin to thwart them. Simply search the Internet for a comment-spam-prevention plugin and install it in the plugin folder of your Wordpress installation. This simple measure is all that is required to take care of this problem.

Commenting on Blogs

You have seen the benefits of interacting with your blog readers via comments, so now let's talk about why you should post comments on blogs within your book's niche. This practice will allow you to connect with bloggers in your genre, it will allow you to offer helpful information to the readers of these similar blogs, and it will help your web site rankings by increasing the number of incoming links to your blog.

When posting comments on blogs be sure that your comment is worthwhile. Never try to sell your book. Instead, just take on the role of the helpful reader who just so happens to be an authority in the field.

Social Networks Where Bibliophiles Can Share Books

It seems like you can't go two seconds without hearing about MySpace, Facebook, or Twitter. Social networking sites seem to be all the rage. Well, luckily for writers, there are five social networking sites (Fig. 21) that are geared specifically toward bibliophiles. They are:

Networking Works

- **Shelfari**
- **BookArmy**
- **LibraryThing**
- **Goodreads**
- **BookJetty**
- **aNobii**

Fig. 21 - LibraryThing

You should sign-up at each of these sites and network with their members. If the site offers the option of creating an author's account, then be sure to take advantage of it as doing so will increase your credibility at the site. Be sure to add some books, including yours, to your virtual shelf, book list, or whatever that particular site calls it. Next, join some groups on the site that are similar to the genre or subject of your book and interact with the group's members.

Once again you want to be helpful and to earn their respect. Become a valued member of the community and you will be rewarded with increased sales.

Get Your Readers All A-Twitter

Twitter is interesting in that it has become an excellent venue for celebrities to connect with their fans. Yes, some celebrities may have joined Twitter just for the sake of being a part of it all, but for others Twitter has become an excellent way to re-enforce their brand and market to the masses. With a simple tweet, they can mass market with news about their latest movie or concert. Some of the most popular celebrities on Twitter have hundreds of thousands of people following their every tweet.

Sure, you may not be as well-known as Dave Matthews and it may be some time before you gather as many followers as Stephen Fry, but that doesn't mean that you shouldn't take advantage of all that Twitter has to offer. Just think how many people that you could reach out to if you were to join the site.

For authors, Twitter is a brilliant opportunity for marketing that really shouldn't be missed. The reason why Twitter is so effective is that it allows you to keep in touch with your readers on anything and everything related to your book. If you have a soon-to-be published guest blog post, then send out a tweet to let your followers know. If you have begun working on your follow-up, then send out a tweet so that your followers can be the first to find out.

Fraternizing in the Forums

Forums on every possible subject abound on the Internet, which is great for you because they are excellent places to promote books. Search Google for forums on subjects similar to your book and then investigate them to see if they are worth your promotional efforts. You can judge their value to your promotional efforts by visiting the forum and seeing how many members that they have. Next, determine if the forum is active. If a forum has too few members or isn't frequently posted to, then you shouldn't waste your time. You are only looking for forums with a large and active membership. Once you find a few suitable forums then join in the conversation.

Now, I should warn you that forums are an easy place to get in an argument. It seems that some forums are just teeming with people who love to fight. I'm not saying that this is the case for every forum, but, in my experience, it goes for quite a lot of them. One thing that seems to cause a lot of trouble is signature files. You should have one. Otherwise, networking in the forum is pointless, but be careful what you put in it. Read the rules of the forum as some do not allow promotional signatures. If you are unsure if your signature would comply with the rules of the forum then post a message and ask the members. This will show them that you are trying to be respectful of the rules that they have set in place.

Should you find that you have landed yourself in an argument then remain professional and do not argue. Realize that the thread will likely go on for pages with posters just fueling the fire. Also, know that you will probably be tempted to continue to defend yourself. You must not, however, give in to that temptation as you might wind up behaving in an unprofessional manner. Just take the high road and people will respect you for it.

It may sound like there is a lot that can go wrong in forums and, really there is, but that doesn't mean that it isn't worth investing time there to network with the other members. Just be cautious and forum participation will prove worthwhile.

Chapter 7

Alternate Formats

It is a simple fact that the more formats that you make your book available in, the greater the odds are that a customer will buy it. As a print-on-demand publisher you should consider making your book available for Kindle, as an ebook, and as an audio book. Luckily, it isn't that much of an undertaking to make your book available in all three formats.

If you want to sell your book on Kindle then you will need to visit the Digital Text Platform page at Amazon. There you will find detailed instructions for turning your print publication into a downloadable Kindle edition.

You should already have the PDF edition of your book that you used to upload to your print-on-demand publisher, but it can't be used to sell an ebook edition. It was formatted for print, which means that the margin will be bigger on one side of every page to accommodate the spine. To handle that problem, open your manuscript in your word processing program and adjust the settings so that the left and right margins are equal. Also, the size of your page will be much smaller than the standard ebook size of 8.5 inches x 11 inches. You can also just go into your settings and change the document size to these larger dimensions. After making these changes, additional formatting may be required. Even so, reformatting your book to sell as an ebook shouldn't be any trouble at all.

In order to sell ebooks from your site, you could simply add a PayPal button, but then you would have to deal with things like automated delivery of files, auto-responses, etc. There is, however, a better alternative called E-junkie. They offer secure download links, discount codes, a shopping cart, the ability to manage affiliates, and much more. You should keep in mind, however, that if you go with E-junkie then you will still need a payment processor i.e. PayPal or Google Checkout. As you can see, PayPal alone doesn't really compare when you see what E-junkie has to offer, but when you combine the two you have a full-fledged sales machine that will work for you 24/7.

Now that we have covered Kindle and ebook editions, let's investigate audio books. The iPod has done wonders for the audio book and POD publishers should seriously consider cashing in. You can either convert your book to audio yourself or outsource the project. Once you have the finished audio file you can also use E-junkie to sell it from your site as well as via the iTunes store.

Chapter 8

Here, There, and Everywhere

After reading all of the information in the previous pages one thing should be clear to you. If you want to be a successful print-on-demand publisher then you have to be here, there, and everywhere. The more places that you and your book are visible, the better your odds are for making sale after sale. Set about to make it so that everywhere a potential buyer turns they encounter your book. The more times that they are exposed to your product, the more likely they will be to buy a copy.

Make an effort everyday to undertake one or more of the promotional techniques outlined in these pages. It doesn't matter which publicity method that you choose on any given day just so long as you set aside the time to garner additional exposure for your title. Post a message to your blog and reply to some comments, write a Listmania! list, do some article marketing, go post in a forum, or work to get a podcast interview. It really doesn't matter just so long as you do something. Before you know it, your book will be visible everywhere and your efforts will be rewarded with a well-read and profitable book.

The most important thing in all of this is to never give up. There may be days when you think that you are never going to succeed in making your book a success, but you just have to keep at it and remain focused. The moment that you stop trying then failure will be guaranteed. As long as you keep trying then success is always possible.

Appendix

Web Site Addresses

Here you will find URLs for the various web sites mentioned throughout this book. Every effort has been made to compile an accurate list of URLs. Please keep in mind, however, that the web is ever changing. While these URLs were accurate at the time that this book was written, they may have changed after publication. Should you find an inaccurate URL then simply search Google and you should locate the web site that you are trying to find.

99 Designs - http://99designs.com

Alexa – http://alexa.com

Amapedia - http://amapedia.amazon.com

Amazon - http://amazon.com

aNobii – http://anobii.com

Author Central – http://authorcentral.amazon.com

Blogger - http://blogger.com

Book Content Update Form - http://amazon.com/gp/content-form/?ie=UTF8&product=books

BookJetty – http://bookjetty.com

CreateSpace - http://createspace.com

Digital Text Platform – http://dtp.amazon.com

E-junkie – http://e-junkie.com

Elance - http://elance.com

Elegant Themes - http://elegantthemes.com

EzineArticles – http://ezinearticles.com

Facebook – http://facebook.com

Feedburner – http://feedburner.com

GoArticles.com – http://goarticles.com

Go Daddy - http://godaddy.com

Goodreads – http://goodreads.com

Google - http://google.com

Google Checkout – http://checkout.google.com

Host Gator - http://hostgator.com

IdeaMarketers – http://ideamarketers.com

LibraryThing – http://librarything.com

Listmania! - http://www.amazon.com/gp/richpub/listmania/createpipeline

Lulu – http://lulu.com

MySpace – http://myspace.com

New York Times, The - http://nytimes.com

PayPal – http://paypal.com

Podcast Pickle - http://podcastpickle.com

Web Site Addresses

Premium Themes - http://premiumthemes.com

Quantcast – http://quantcast.com

RefDesk - http://www.refdesk.com/paper.html

Rent a Coder - http://rentacoder.com

Reseller Zoom - http://resellerzoom.com

Shelfari – http://shelfari.com

So You'd Like to... - http://www.amazon.com/gp/richpub/syltguides/create

Target – http://target.com

Technorati Top 100 - http://technorati.com/pop/blogs/

ThemeForest – http://themeforest.net

Twitter – http://twitter.com

USA Today - http://usatoday.com

Wikipedia.com – http://wikipedia.com

Wordpress.com - http://wordpress.com

Index

99 Designs................14
Add more books..............44
Affiliates................115
Alexa rating................72
Amapedia................56
Amazon account................41
Amazon reviewers................91
Amazon Search................48
Amazon.com................37
AmazonConnect................41
aNobii................107
Article marketing................97
Article repositories................100
Audio book................113
Author biography.....34, 39, 45
Author Central................41
Author Central blog................45
Author comments................39
Author photo................33, 45
Author profile page................45
Back cover copy................17, 39
Bibliography................43
Blog................20
Blog comments................104
Blogger................22
Blogger theme................26
Blurbs................35
Book Content Update Form 39
Book cover................12, 33
Book detail page................39
BookArmy................107
BookJetty................107
Buy X, Get Y................56
Checklist................71
Circulation................75
Claim your books................43
Comments................104, 105
community-help@amazon.com................61
Contact information................35
Cover letter................67
CreateSpace................5
CreateSpace Pro Plan................7
Crowdsourcing................14
Customer Communities................59
Customer Image Gallery................58
Customer reviews................34
Damaged book................64
Description................39
Design contest................14
Digital Text Platform page 113
Domain name................23
Domain registrar................23
Duplicate content................45
E-junkie................114
Ebook................63, 113
Elance................14
Elegant Themes................29
Excerpts................34, 39
Expert status................90, 98
EzineArticles................101
Facebook................106
Fantastico................25
FAQs................36
Feedburner................75
Feedburner FeedCount Chicklet................75
Feedburner subscribers................75

Follow-up................................84	Poynter, Dan...........................i
Formats................................113	Premium Blogger theme.....26
Forums................................110	Premium Themes.................29
Go Daddy..............................23	Premium Wordpress theme
Go Daddy Domain Manager 23	26
	Press release...................32, 95
GoArticles............................101	Proof copy..............................5
Goodreads...........................107	Publicity................................63
Google..............................68, 87	Publisher's comments..........39
Google Checkout.................115	Quantcast.............................73
Guest blogging.....................90	*Que's Internet Yellow Pages*. 5
Host Gator............................25	RefDesk................................70
IdeaMarketers....................101	Rent a Coder........................14
Incoming links....................106	Resales.................................64
Inside flap copy.....................39	Reseller Zoom......................24
International publishers........6	Resource box........................97
Interview........................80, 87	Respectability........................8
iTunes...........................88, 115	Review slip............................65
Kindle..................................113	Reviewer package................64
LibraryThing.......................107	Reviews..........33, 39, 60, 68, 91
Link popularity.....................98	RSS feed..........................45, 75
Listmania!.............................49	Rubber stamp......................65
Lulu..5	Sample email............80, 84, 89
Magazines.............................75	Search Inside.......................46
Media kit 31	Self-publishing......................1
MySpace..............................106	*Self-Publishing Manual, The*.1
Negative reviews..................61	*She-Commerce*.....................v
Networking.........................103	Shelfari...............................107
New York Times, The...........70	Signature file......................111
Newspapers....................70, 75	So You'd Like to...Guides.....52
Notable reviews....................33	Social networking...............106
Online marketplace..............12	Social networks..................106
Outsourcing..........................14	Spreadsheet...................77, 88
Paid placement.....................56	Static web site......................20
PayPal.................................114	Suggest product information updates..................................44
Podcast Pickle......................88	
Podcasters...........................87	Table of contents..................39
Podcasts...............................87	Tags..........................47, 51, 53

124

Index

Technorati Top 100 70
Testimonials 40
ThemeForest 29
Title 15
Traditional publishing 1
Twitter 108
URLs 119
USA Today 70
Web hosting 24
Web presence 19
Wikipedia 75
Wordpress 25
Wordpress theme 26
Wordpress.com 22
Writing reviews 60

Made in the USA
Lexington, KY
28 July 2011